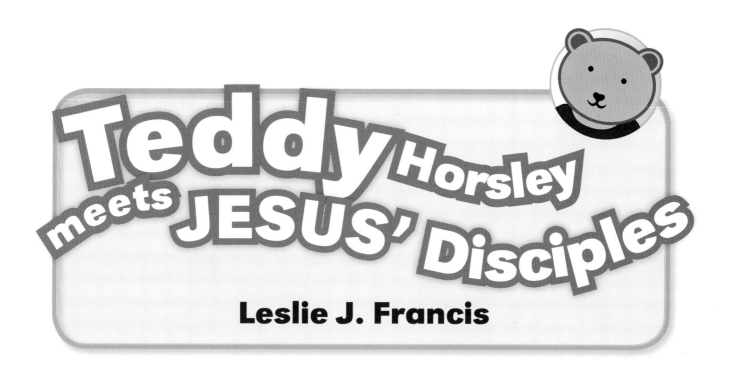

Teddy Horsley meets JESUS' Disciples

Leslie J. Francis

The Bear facts

Teddy Horsley and Betsy Bear are part of a churchgoing family. They live with Lucy, Walter, and Mr and Mrs Henry. The Teddy Horsley books are designed to build bridges between the young child's day-to-day experiences of the world and major biblical themes and stories. The series is a result of extensive research into the religious development of young children, and the author's wide experience of educational work in schools and churches.

Leslie J. Francis is Director of the Welsh National Centre for Religious Education and Professor of Practical Theology at University of Wales, Bangor.

Text copyright © Leslie J. Francis 2006
Illustrations copyright © Phillip Vernon 2006

Published 2006 by CWR, Waverley Abbey House, Waverley Lane, Farnham, Surrey GU9 8EP, England.

The right of Leslie J. Francis to be identified as the author of this work has been asserted by him in accordance with the Copyright, Designs and Patents Act 1988.

See back of book for list of National Distributors.

Unless otherwise indicated, all Scripture references are from the Good News Bible, copyright © American Bible Society 1966, 1971, 1976, 1992, 1994.

Concept development, editing, design and production by CWR.

Printed in Slovenia by Compass Press.

ISBN-13: 978-1-85345-396-0
ISBN-10: 1-85345-396-X

Other titles featuring Teddy Horsley and Betsy Bear, published by Christian Education, include:

Autumn
Do and Tell
Explorer
Hide and Seek
Lights
Music Makers
Neighbours
Night Time
People Everywhere
The Broken Leg
The Craft Show
The Grumpy Day
The Picnic
The Present
The Rainy Day
The Song
The Walk
The Windy Day
Water

It is Sunday morning and Teddy Horsley is a very excited bear.

On Sunday morning Teddy Horsley gets up early and goes out with Lucy, Walter and Betsy Bear.

Mr and Mrs Henry lead Teddy Horsley past the shops until they come to the church. What will be happening there this week?

Teddy Horsley and Betsy Bear meet with their friends to take part in a play about Jesus' disciples.

Today they choose costumes to become fishermen, tax collectors, carpenters, farmers, and even Jesus Himself.

The story all began when Jesus was walking beside the Sea of Galilee. He saw boats and fishermen busy at work.

Some were mending boats. Some were selling fish. Some were telling tales of storms and of catches beyond belief.

Simon and his brother Andrew were busy casting their net into the lake, seeking a catch of fish.

Jesus called them, 'Come, follow Me. I will make you fishers of people.' Simon and Andrew came. Now there were two disciples.

James and his brother John, the sons of Zebedee, were busy mending their nets, ready to set out on the lake.

Jesus called them, 'Come, follow Me. I will make you fishers of people.' James and John came. Now there were four disciples.

Soon after they had been called Jesus took these four disciples into the synagogue on the Sabbath. There Jesus began to teach.

The four disciples were amazed at what they heard, since Jesus taught with such authority and power.

Inside the synagogue there was a man possessed by an evil spirit. There Jesus began to cure the sick.

The four disciples were amazed at what they saw, since even evil spirits obeyed Jesus' commands.

The story developed when Jesus was walking past the tax office set up by the Roman army.

There in the tax office Jesus saw the tax collectors busy at work, raising money to feed the soldiers.

Levi, the son of Alphaeus, was busy counting out the money he had collected, hoping for a rich profit.

Jesus called him, 'Come, follow Me. I will give you a new start in life.' Now there were five disciples.

Soon after they had been called Jesus took these five disciples to Levi's house for dinner, and they heard the conversation.

The five disciples were amazed to hear Jesus say, 'I have not come to call the righteous, but sinners.'

The story continued when Jesus went up into the hills and called to Him those He wanted to be disciples and apostles.

Jesus called Philip and Bartholomew, Matthew and Thomas, James and Thaddaeus, Simon and Judas. Now there were twelve disciples.

The story continues today when Jesus walks through our world and continues with His call, 'Come, follow Me.'

Men and women, boys and girls, leave their busy work to follow where Jesus leads. Now there are millions of disciples.

It is Sunday morning and Teddy Horsley has heard Jesus' call, 'Come, follow Me'.

As Jesus walked along the shore of Lake Galilee, he saw two fishermen, Simon and his brother Andrew, catching fish with a net. Jesus said to them, 'Come with me, and I will teach you to catch people.' At once they left their nets and went with him.

He went a little farther on and saw two other brothers, James and John, the sons of Zebedee. They were in their boat getting their nets ready. As soon as Jesus saw them, he called them; they left their father Zebedee in the boat with the hired men and went with Jesus.

Mark 1:16–20

Jesus went back again to the shore of Lake Galilee. A crowd came to him, and he started teaching them. As he walked along, he saw a tax collector, Levi son of Alphaeus, sitting in his office. Jesus said to him, 'Follow me.' Levi got up and followed him.

Mark 2:13–14

These questions suggest further ways
of developing links between the young
child's experience, the story and the
Bible passage.

Talk about friends:
Who are your friends?
What are their names?
What other names do you know?

Talk about Jesus' friends:
Who were Jesus' friends?
What are their names?
How did Jesus meet His friends?

Talk about fishermen:
Have you been to the seaside?
Have you seen fishing boats?
What do fishermen do?

Talk about the story:
What were Peter and Andrew doing?
What were James and John doing?
What was Levi doing?

Think some more about the story:
Who would you want to be in the play?
How would you like to follow Jesus?
Who are Jesus' friends today?

National Distributors

UK: (and countries not listed below)
CWR, Waverley Abbey House, Waverley Lane, Farnham, Surrey GU9 8EP.
Tel: (01252) 784700 Outside UK (+44) 1252 784700

AUSTRALIA: CMC Australasia, PO Box 519, Belmont, Victoria 3216.
Tel: (03) 5241 3288 Fax: (03) 5241 3290

CANADA: Cook Communications Ministries, PO Box 98, 55 Woodslee Avenue, Paris, Ontario N3L 3E5.
Tel: 1800 263 2664

GHANA: Challenge Enterprises of Ghana, PO Box 5723, Accra.
Tel: (021) 222437/223249 Fax: (021) 226227

HONG KONG: Cross Communications Ltd, 1/F, 562A Nathan Road, Kowloon.
Tel: 2780 1188 Fax: 2770 6229

INDIA: Crystal Communications, 10-3-18/4/1, East Marredpalli, Secunderabad – 500026,
Andhra Pradesh.
Tel/Fax: (040) 27737145

KENYA: Keswick Books and Gifts Ltd, PO Box 10242, Nairobi.
Tel: (02) 331692/226047 Fax: (02) 728557

MALAYSIA: Salvation Book Centre (M) Sdn Bhd, 23 Jalan SS 2/64, 47300 Petaling Jaya, Selangor.
Tel: (03) 78766411/78766797 Fax: (03) 78757066/78756360

NEW ZEALAND: CMC Australasia, PO Box 36015, Lower Hutt.
Tel: 0800 449 408 Fax: 0800 449 049

NIGERIA: FBFM, Helen Baugh House, 96 St Finbarr's College Road, Akoka, Lagos.
Tel: (01) 7747429/4700218/825775/827264

PHILIPPINES: OMF Literature Inc, 776 Boni Avenue, Mandaluyong City.
Tel: (02) 531 2183 Fax: (02) 531 1960

SINGAPORE: Armour Publishing Pte Ltd, Block 203A Henderson Road,
11–06 Henderson Industrial Park, Singapore 159546.
Tel: 6 276 9976 Fax: 6 276 7564

SOUTH AFRICA: Struik Christian Books, 80 MacKenzie Street, PO Box 1144, Cape Town 8000.
Tel: (021) 462 4360 Fax: (021) 461 3612

SRI LANKA: Christombu Publications (Pvt) Ltd., Bartleet House, 65 Braybrooke Place,
Colombo 2. Tel: (01) 433142/328909

TANZANIA: CLC Christian Book Centre, PO Box 1384, Mkwepu Street, Dar es Salaam.
Tel/Fax: (022) 2119439

USA: Cook Communications Ministries, PO Box 98, 55 Woodslee Avenue, Paris, Ontario N3L 3E5, Canada.
Tel: 1800 263 2664

ZIMBABWE: Word of Life Books (Pvt) Ltd, Christian Media Centre, 8 Aberdeen Road, Avondale,
PO Box A480 Avondale, Harare.
Tel: (04) 333355 or 091301188

For email addresses, visit the CWR website: www.cwr.org.uk
CWR is a registered charity – Number 294387
CWR is a limited company registered in England – Registration Number 1990308

These titles published by **Christian Education**

www.christianeducation.org.uk

A Teddy Horsley Book
The Sunny Morning
Teddy Horsley celebrates the new life of Easter

A Teddy Horsley Book
The Broken Leg
Teddy Horsley meets Jesus in all who help him

A Teddy Horsley Book
The Windy Day
Teddy Horsley and the Holy Spirit

A Teddy Horsley Book
The Present
Betsy Bear meets the Three Men